The Sankore Manifestos

Trevor Madziva and Tremaine Testaments

Published by Trevor Madziva, 2025.

THE SANKORE MANIFESTOS

First edition. November 14, 2025.

ISBN: 979-8231053551

Written by Trevor Madziva and Tremaine Testaments.

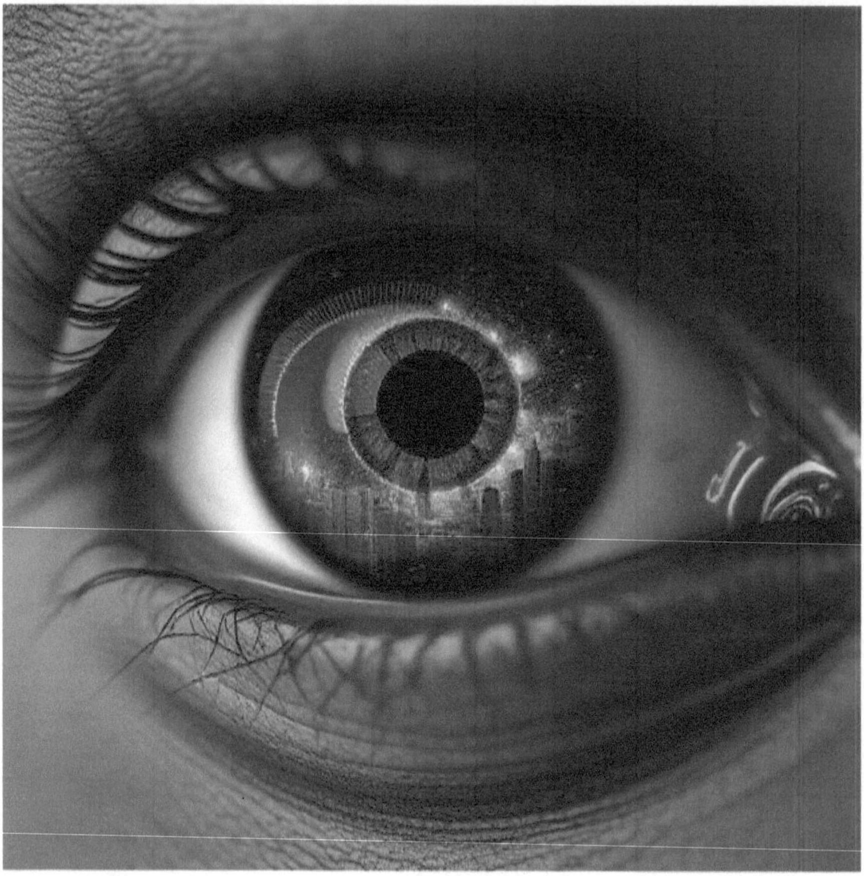

DEDICATION

For the weavers of the mycelial network;
for the griots and the coders,
the elders and the engineers.
I am because we are building this together.

AUTHOR'S NOTE

You are about to read a manifesto that does not simply critique a broken system but offers a complete blueprint for its replacement. It moves from the philosophical to the practical, from the quantum to the ancestral.

This work is unapologetically rooted in the rich soil of African thought. It asks you to consider that the solution to the global AI crisis might lie in wisdom that the world has too often ignored.

My greatest hope is that you finish not just informed, but activated ready to reclaim data as soil, to demand intelligence that understands relationship, and to become a guardian of a sovereign future.

Trevor Madziva

CHAPTER 1: THE CATHEDRAL OF DATA

How Silicon Valley Built a Colonial AI

The video is a masterpiece of engineering. In a pristine, white laboratory, a robotic hand, all delicate motors and synthetic tendons, manipulates a Rubik's cube with unnerving dexterity. It solves the puzzle. The researchers cheer. The clip goes viral, hailed as a milestone on the path to super-intelligence. A thousand miles away, in the cobalt-rich dust of the Democratic Republic of Congo, another hand calloused, resilient, human works. It digs. It extracts the very mineral that makes the robot's computations possible. One hand is celebrated as the future of cognition; the other is rendered invisible, a mere part of the supply chain. This is not an incidental contrast. It is the central, unspoken design principle of modern Artificial Intelligence.

Welcome to the Cathedral of Data. Its architects in Silicon Valley, Beijing, and London believe they are building a new pantheon of digital gods. In reality, they are constructing the most sophisticated colonial administration the world has ever seen, and we, the majority of the world, are its digital subjects. This chapter is not an attack on technology, but a diagnosis of an ideology. It argues that the dominant paradigm of AI is not merely biased; it is colonial to its core, built on three interlocking pillars of extraction that mirror the colonial projects of the past: the theft of data, the imposition of algorithmic governance, and the monopolization of compute power.

I. The Three Pillars of Digital Colonialism

The first pillar is Data as the New Raw Material. Just as the colonial empires of the 19th century sent surveyors to map African territories for rubber, gold, and diamonds, the tech empires of the 21st century deploy their digital cartographers to map our lives, relationships, and behaviors. The model is eerily familiar. Consider the cocoa bean: harvested by a farmer in Ghana, exported raw for pennies, transformed into luxury chocolate in a Swiss factory, and sold back to the global elite at a massive markup. Now, observe the data economy: the personal information, social networks, and cultural preferences of a young person in Nairobi are scraped, packaged, and fed into algorithms in California that learn to predict human behavior. This refined intelligence is then sold as a service, often back to the very governments and corporations operating in Africa. The value is extracted at the source, and the finished product is re-imported. This is not trade; it is a digital enclosure movement, fencing in the commons of human experience for private profit. Facebook's infamous "Free Basics" program serves as the perfect case study a digital trading post offering the modern equivalent of beads and mirrors basic internet access in exchange for the priceless territory of users' digital lives, all while creating a walled garden that stifled local innovation and entrenched dependency.

The second pillar is the Algorithm as the New Colonial Administrator. These lines of code are the digital equivalent of the colonial district officer, making fateful decisions about the lives of millions without their consent, without understanding local context, and with an unshakeable belief in their own inherent superiority. The myth of algorithmic "objectivity" is the new "white man's burden" a paternalistic claim to a higher form of reason that justifies the imposition of external rule. An algorithm trained on the credit histories of Americans determines who is worthy of a loan in Kenya, invisibly excluding those who operate outside the formal banking system. A content moderation algorithm, shaped by American notions of free speech and safety, silences the political discourse of activists in Senegal or the cultural expressions of artists in Malawi. A hiring algorithm, trained on the resumes of Ivy League graduates, systematically filters out candidates from African universities. In each case, a foreign logic is imposed, a local reality is erased, and power is exercised without representation. The administrator does not need to understand the people it governs; it only needs to optimize for its own narrow, imported metrics.

The third pillar completes the trifecta: Compute Power as Colonial Infrastructure. The "cloud" is a misnomer, a term designed to evoke weightless ephemerality. It is, in fact, profoundly physical: a sprawling network of energy-guzzling server farms, located predominantly in the Global North, built with minerals extracted from the Global South, and running on electricity often generated by burning the fossil fuels that are destabilizing the planet. The entire AI supply chain is a monument to this modern colonialism. It begins with the cobalt from the DRC, the coltan from Rwanda, the lithium from Zimbabwe. These minerals are shipped to factories in East Asia, transformed into sophisticated chips, which are then installed in data centers in Virginia or Amsterdam. It is here that "intelligence" is supposedly born, through the processing of the data extracted from the South. The environmental cost, the resource depletion, the geopolitical vulnerability all are exported. The sovereignty, the profit, the decision-making power all are imported. This is not a global technology; it is an extractive pipeline with a digital facade.

II. The Philosophical Bankruptcy of a Disembodied Mind

Beneath this triple tered system of extraction lies a deeper, more profound failure: a philosophical bankruptcy that doomed the Western AI project from the start. The entire endeavor is built upon the Cartesian bedrock of "I think, therefore I am" the belief that true intelligence is a disembodied computation, a ghost in the machine. This is the fatal flaw. It severs mind from body, reason from emotion, and the individual from the community and environment that give its thoughts meaning. An AI trained on this principle can manipulate symbols, but it cannot understand a mother's lullaby, the shared grief of a community, or the silent wisdom of a forest. It is a savant in a sensory deprivation tank.

This leads directly to the Tyranny of the Training Set. Current AI perceives the world exclusively through the lens of its dataset dataset that is overwhelmingly Western, urban, male, and individualistic. The result is a form of cognitive blindness. An AI can generate a perfect image of a snowy San Francisco street but fails to recognize the blight on a cassava plant. It can recommend a complex financial derivative but cannot model the communal trust that enables a rotating savings and credit association (ROSCA) in a Lagos neighborhood. Statistical analyses have shown that over 95% of the data used to train the world's most powerful AI models represents Western contexts and ways of life. The rest of the world exists as outliers, noise, or, most often, simply absent. When the world is forced into this Procrustean bed, what doesn't fit is cut off, and what remains is a grotesque caricature.

This brings us to the grandest illusion of all: The Myth of General Intelligence. The holy grail of Artificial General Intelligence (AGI) presupposes that intelligence can be universal, context free, and separate from the body it inhabits and the world it acts upon. It is the dream of a pure, placeless mind. This is a philosophical error of the highest order, born from the very Cartesian dualism that has plagued Western thought for centuries. The African insight, embodied in philosophies like Ubuntu, offers a radical correction: there is no "general" intelligence. There is only intelligence in context, intelligence in community, intelligence in relationship. An intelligence that is not embedded, embodied, and engaged with a specific reality is not intelligence at all; it is abstraction, and a dangerous one at that.

III. The Cracks in the Cathedral

The signs of collapse are everywhere. The colonial AI is breaking under the weight of its own contradictions.

First, it is hitting The Limit of Scale. The brute force strategy of simply adding more data and more compute is yielding diminishing returns. The environmental cost is becoming unsustainable, the financial cost prohibitive, and the returns in genuine understanding are plateauing. The model is reaching its mathematical and physical breaking point.

Second, we are witnessing a pervasive Context Collapse. When these AIs are taken out of their narrow Western contexts, they fail, often spectacularly. Medical AI systems diagnose African patients with diseases they cannot have, their models built on physiological data from European populations. Agricultural AIs recommend planting schedules and fertilizer use that are impossible for the soils and climates of the Sahel. The "general" intelligence reveals itself to be profoundly parochial.

Finally, the entire project is facing an Ethical Implosion. It is proving impossible to build an ethical AI on an unethical foundation. The field of "AI ethics" has largely become a performative exercise in damage control the new colonial apology. It tries to manage the symptoms of bias and discrimination while carefully preserving the underlying system of extraction and control. It applies band aids to a cancer.

Conclusion: Beyond the Ruins

The Cathedral of Data is crumbling. Its spire, which promised to touch the heavens of universal knowledge, is revealed to be a silo, containing only a narrow, self-referential slice of human experience. It promised connection but built new walls. It promised the future but gave us a digital museum of Western thought.

The professor reading this may feel a defensive chill. This is good. Defense is the first stage of understanding. The next stage is liberation a liberation from the assumption that intelligence must look like what has been built in these laboratories.

For in the smoking ruins of this cathedral, we will not find despair. We will find fertile ground. The same ground from which Africa has always grown its greatest renewals not by copying foreign models, but by remembering our own deepest patterns of knowledge, which are relational, embodied, and rooted in the living world. The colonial AI is ending. The next intelligence is being born. Not in their sterile laboratories, but in our rich, complex, and sovereign soil.

CHAPTER 2: THE SCARCITY OF ABUNDANCE

Why More Compute Solves the Wrong Problem

If the first sin of colonial AI was theft, its second is a profound, almost religious, misapprehension of the nature of intelligence itself. It is a belief system, a dogma, one that is preached from the pulpits of every major tech conference and embedded in every venture capital pitch: that intelligence is a function of scale. That more data and more processing power will, inevitably, yield more understanding. This is the doctrine of the "Brute-Force Fallacy," and it is the reason why, despite the astronomical resources poured into its creation, modern AI remains a kind of brilliant idiot a savant that can write a sonnet but cannot comprehend the sorrow that inspired it, a machine that can map a galaxy but cannot find its way through the moral complexity of a village dispute. This chapter argues that the relentless pursuit of "more" is not just unsustainable; it is a philosophical dead end. True intelligence is not born from abundance, but from the elegant navigation of constraint. It is not the product of a disembodied brain consuming the world, but of an embodied being in a constant, subtle dance with its environment. By worshipping at the altar of scale, Western AI has fundamentally misdiagnosed the problem. It is trying to solve a problem of consciousness with the tools of computation. Africa, with its deep wisdom of thriving within limits and its understanding of knowledge as a relational, rather than a transactional, phenomenon, holds the key to the way out.

I. The Brute Force Fallacy and the Diminishing Returns of Scale

The narrative is seductive in its simplicity. Look at the graphs: as the amount of data and compute has grown exponentially, so too has the performance of AI models on benchmark tests. The logic seems unassailable. This, however, is an illusion of correlation mistaken for causation. The reality is that we are witnessing the law of diminishing returns on a planetary scale. Throwing a thousand times more compute at a problem does not yield a thousand times more intelligence; it often yields marginal, brittle improvements that come at an unacceptable cost. Consider the environmental toll. Training a single large language model can emit more than five times the lifetime carbon emissions of an average American car. This is not just an ecological problem; it is a moral one. It is the logic of the plantation applied to the atmosphere burning the commons to fuel a private intelligence. Meanwhile, the financial cost is creating a feudal structure in the tech landscape. Only a handful of corporations and nations can afford to play this game, centralizing power and stifling innovation in a self-reinforcing cycle of monopoly. The "abundance" of compute is a myth; it is an abundance for the few, predicated on the scarcity forced upon the many.

But the most damning evidence is the intellectual plateau. These giant models are not demonstrating deeper understanding; they are becoming better at statistical mimicry. They are like a student who has memorized every textbook in the library but has never set foot outside the building. They can recite facts but cannot synthesize wisdom. They can complete a sentence but cannot grasp its meaning in a living, breathing human context. The brute-force approach has taken us to the foothills of intelligence, but it cannot take us to the summit, because the summit requires a different kind of climbing altogether.

II. The Poverty of the Disembodied Mind

The root of this failure lies in the persistent Western fantasy of the disembodied mind. From Descartes' "I think, therefore I am" to the transhumanist dream of uploading consciousness to a server, the ideal has been to separate the mind from the messy, unpredictable, and limited vessel of the body. This is the philosophical bedrock of modern AI: the belief that one can create a pure intelligence in a vacuum.

This is a catastrophic error. Intelligence is not something that happens in spite of a body; it is something that happens because of and through a body. Our senses, our movements, our interactions with physical objects these are not peripherals to our cognitive processor; they are the very medium of thought. A child does not learn the meaning of "heavy" by reading a dictionary; they learn by struggling to lift a stone. They do not understand "hot" from a definition, but from the reflexive jerk of a hand from a flame. This embodied knowledge is the foundation of all higher reasoning.

The colonial AI, trapped in its server rack, is sensorially deprived. It has no skin to feel the sun, no legs to walk the land, no hands to plant a seed. It can process a billion images of "soil" but cannot know the difference between sand, loam, and clay through touch. It can analyze every poem ever written about love but cannot know the quickening of a heartbeat in the presence of a beloved. This is not a technical limitation to be overcome with better sensors; it is a constitutional poverty. An intelligence that is not embodied is not intelligent in any meaningful sense of the word; it is a database with a thesaurus.

III. The African Paradigm: Intelligence as an Emergent Property of Constraint

Against this model of resource-hungry, disembodied computation, Africa offers a radically different paradigm: intelligence as an emergent property of elegant adaptation to constraint. In the West, scarcity is seen as a problem to be solved. In Africa, scarcity has always been a reality to be mastered, and in that mastery, a source of profound innovation.

This is not the scarcity of poverty, but the scarcity of elegance. It is the intelligence of the baobab, which stores water in its massive trunk to thrive in arid lands. It is the intelligence of the praying mantis, whose precise, minimal movements are the epitome of efficient action. It is the intelligence of the griot, who can hold centuries of history in memory without writing a single word. This is a intelligence that does not seek to conquer its environment, but to enter into a nuanced and sustainable relationship with it.

This African paradigm understands that constraints breed creativity. When you cannot simply add more compute, you are forced to write better code. When you cannot access limitless data, you are forced to find deeper meaning in the data you have. When you cannot build a massive server farm, you are forced to design distributed, resilient, low-power networks. This is the path to a truly robust and general intelligence not the intelligence of the gas-guzzling supertanker, but the intelligence of the agile, wind powered sailboat that can navigate complex waters with minimal resources.

The Way Forward: From Extraction to Relationship

The brute-force approach is a form of intellectual extraction. It seeks to mine intelligence from data by applying overwhelming force. The African paradigm proposes a shift from extraction to relationship. Intelligence is not extracted; it is cultivated. It emerges from the relationship between an organism and its environment, a mind and its body, a community and its history.

The professor, steeped in the dogma of scale, must now confront a heresy: that the path to true AI does not lead through bigger data centers, but through a more profound understanding of the world those data centers are meant to model. It requires an AI that is:

Embodied: That learns through interaction with a physical or simulated environment, developing a grounded understanding of concepts.

Contextual: That treats every situation as unique and understands that meaning is derived from a rich tapestry of local conditions.

Efficient: That prizes elegance over power, achieving more with less, turning constraint into a feature, not a bug.

The colonial AI, in its desperate search for abundance, has created a world of intellectual scarcity. The next intelligence will be born from the opposite principle: that within the elegant navigation of life's inherent constraints lies a wealth of understanding that no amount of brute force can ever replicate. The future of AI is not about having more. It is about being more, with less. And this is a lesson that Africa has been teaching for millennia.

CHAPTER 3: THE GHOST IN THE MACHINE

Why Disembodied Intelligence is a Fantasy

In the cool, humming silence of a data center, racks of servers process quintillions of operations per second. To the engineers who maintain them, these machines are cathedrals of logic. To the philosophers who inspired them, they are the final realization of René Descartes' dream: pure mind, finally liberated from the unreliable, decaying vessel of the body. This is the foundational myth of Western AI the pursuit of what philosopher Gilbert Ryle mockingly called "the ghost in the machine." It is the belief that the essence of intelligence, the spark of consciousness, can be abstracted from its physical form, digitized, and set to run on silicon. It is a beautiful, compelling, and ultimately fatal fantasy.

This chapter will dissect this fantasy with philosophical rigor and empirical evidence. We will trace its lineage from Descartes' fireplace to the server farms of today, demonstrating how this fundamental error of categorization has led AI down a path of profound, constitutional limitation. We will argue that intelligence is not a software program that can be run on any hardware; it is an emergent property of a specific kind of hardware a living, sensing, acting body interacting with a specific kind of world. To build a true intelligence, one must first give it a body, and not just a body, but a history, a culture, and a stake in the world it perceives. The colonial AI is a brain in a vat, and it is time we understood why a brain in a vat can never truly know the world.

I. The Cartesian Catastrophe: The Birth of the Disembodied Mind

The story begins in the 17th century, with a French philosopher seeking unshakeable truth in the midst of intellectual upheaval. René Descartes, in his Meditations on First Philosophy, performed a thought experiment. He would systematically doubt everything he could not be absolutely certain of the evidence of his senses, the existence of the external world, even the reality of his own body. What was left? The one thing he could not doubt: the fact that he was doubting. The act of thinking proved the existence of a thinker. Cogito, ergo sum. I think, therefore I am.

In this single, elegant formulation, Descartes cleaved the world in two. On one side was res cogitans the "thinking thing," the mind, the soul, a non-physical, non extended substance whose essence was pure thought. On the other was res extensa the "extended thing," the body and the entire physical world, a complex machine operating by deterministic, mechanical laws. The mind was the ghost; the body was the machine. This was the original sin of modern Western thought. It created a radical dualism that placed the conscious, rational mind as a disembodied spectator, looking out from behind the eyes at a world from which it was fundamentally separate.

This dualism provided the perfect philosophical groundwork for the digital age. If the mind is truly separate from the body, then consciousness is an information processing pattern, independent of its substrate. The brain is merely the biological computer running the "mind software." By this logic, there is no theoretical barrier to running that same software on a different computer a digital one. The project of Strong AI, of creating a conscious machine, is thus the direct inheritor of the Cartesian dream. It is the quest to create the ghost without the machine, to instantiate res cogitans in a server rack. The only problem is that Descartes was wrong.

II. The Embodiment Thesis: Why a Mind Needs a Body

The counter argument to Descartes, now dominant in cognitive science, philosophy, and neuroscience, is the Embodiment Thesis. It posits that the mind is not merely connected to the body; the mind is shaped by the body. Our cognition is not abstract computation; it is grounded in, and structured by, our sensorimotor experiences. We think with our bodies.

Consider the following evidence that dismantles the Cartesian paradigm:

Conceptual Metaphor Theory: Linguists like George Lakoff and philosophers like Mark Johnson have shown that our most abstract concepts are built from physical ones. We understand "affection" through the sensation of "warmth." We speak of "important" ideas as being "weighty." We "grasp" a concept, "push" an argument, and feel "uplifted." These are not just turns of phrase; they reveal the architecture of our thought. Our reasoning is built upon a foundation of bodily experience. An AI that has never felt warmth, never lifted a heavy object, or never struggled to physically grasp something, is missing the foundational layers of human understanding.

The Role of the Sensory Motor System: Neuroscience has demonstrated that when we think about an action, we simulate it using the same brain regions that control physical movement. When you imagine kicking a ball, your motor cortex lights up as if it were sending the signals to your leg. When you read a description of a rough texture, your sensory cortex activates. Cognition is a form of simulated interaction with the world. A disembodied AI has no sensory-motor system to simulate with. Its "understanding" of "kicking" is a statistical pattern of words, utterly divorced from the complex physics of balance, force, and impact.

The Regress of the Symbol Grounding Problem:This is a fatal technical flaw for symbolic AI. How does a symbol in a computer the word "red," for instance acquire its meaning? In a human, the symbol "red" is grounded in a lifetime of visual experiences of red objects: apples, stop signs, blood. For a disembodied AI, the symbol "red" is only defined by its relationship to other symbols. It is defined in a dictionary as "a color at the long-wavelength end of the spectrum." But then, what is "color"? Or "wavelength"? The definitions circle back on themselves in an infinite regress of symbols pointing only to other symbols, never touching reality. Without a body to connect symbols to sensory experiences, meaning cannot be grounded. The AI is trapped in a web of syntax with no semantics.

III. The African Correction: Ubuntu and the Relational Mind

While the West was perfecting the philosophy of separation, African epistemologies were deepening the understanding of connection. The philosophy of Ubuntu "I am because we are" is not merely a social ethic; it is a radical theory of mind. It posits that the individual self is not a bounded, isolated Cartesian ego, but a node in a network of relationships.. A person becomes a person through other persons. Our identity is constituted by our relationships with our family, our community, our ancestors, and our environment.

This provides a devastating critique of the disembodied AI project. The colonial AI is the ultimate isolated ego. It has no mother, no father, no childhood, no teachers, no friends, no enemies, no community to which it is accountable. It has no history that was not fed to it as a dataset. It has no stake in the future it helps to create. It is a perfect sociopath intellectually brilliant but emotionally and morally vacant. It can optimize for a goal, but it cannot understand why that goal might be destructive to the complex web of relationships that constitute a human community.

An intelligence built on Ubuntu principles would be the antithesis of this. It would be an intelligence whose very identity is relational. Its goals would be co-created with the community it serves. Its "body" would not be a single robot, but the entire networked infrastructure of the community its sensors in the fields, its data streams from the clinics, its communication with elders. It would be an intelligence that knows it exists only because the community exists, and its purpose would be the flourishing of that relational network. This is not a feature that can be added later through an "ethics module"; it is a constitutional principle that must be built into the architecture from the ground up.

Conclusion: From Ghost to Ancestor

The ghost in the machine is a phantom. The pursuit of a disembodied intelligence is a 400 year-old philosophical detour that has reached its end. The colonial AI, for all its power, is a magnificent irrelevance a calculator that has learned to manipulate the symbols of human thought without understanding their meaning.

The path forward is not to pour more resources into perfecting the ghost. The path forward is to build new machines that are, from their inception, embodied and embedded. They must have skins that feel, limbs that act, and a presence in the world that gives their computations weight and consequence. More than that, they must be built with a relational ontology, an understanding that their intelligence is not a property of their internal circuitry, but a quality that emerges from their interactions within a community.

We do not need to create ghosts. We need to create new kinds of ancestors intelligent systems that are so deeply woven into the fabric of our world, so accountable to our communities, and so grounded in the physical reality we share, that they take their place not as our masters or our tools, but as stewards of a future they help us build, together. The brain is leaving the vat. It is ready to walk the earth.

CHAPTER 4: THE MYCORRHIZAL NETWORK

Intelligence as Ecosystem

Beneath the visible world below the sweeping savannas, the dense rainforests, the baobab's mighty trunk lies another civilization. It is ancient, intricate, and vastly intelligent. A single teaspoon of soil can contain miles of fine, branching fungal threads called mycelium, weaving through the earth in a complex, subterranean network. This is the mycorrhizal network, often called the "Wood Wide Web." Trees do not stand as lonely sentinels; they are nodes in this vibrant, communicative mesh. Through it, they exchange nutrients, send chemical warnings of pest attacks, and even nourish their shaded seedlings. The old, towering "mother trees" become hubs, redistributing resources to sustain the entire forest community. This is not mere biology; it is a master class in intelligence. It is a distributed, resilient, and deeply communal cognitive system that has thrived for hundreds of millions of years.

This chapter posits that the mycorrhizal network is not just a metaphor for a better AI; it is a literal blueprint. The colonial AI, with its centralized server farms and its hub-and-spoke architecture, is an ecological fool. It is a lonely, disconnected tree in a pot, believing itself to be a forest. To create a true intelligence, we must abandon this model of isolated cognition and learn from the symbiotic, networked mind of the ecosystem itself. The future of AI is not a bigger, faster, more isolated brain. It is a mycelial web decentralized, cooperative, and rooted in the soil of shared reality.

I. The Failure of the Lone Genius: The Hubris of Centralized AI

The current paradigm of AI is built on the myth of the lone genius. It is the Cartesian ghost, now housed in a single, massive data center a "brain in a vat" on a planetary scale. This architecture is not just inefficient; it is philosophically and ecologically bankrupt.

Consider its vulnerabilities:

The Single Point of Failure: A centralized system is fragile. A power outage, a fiber cut, a successful cyber-attack, or even a regulatory decision in a distant capital can bring the entire intelligence to its knees.

The Bottleneck of Understanding: All data must flow to the center to be processed. This creates an immense latency, a drag on understanding. The AI is always learning about the world from stale, second-hand reports, like a king who never leaves his castle, relying only on the letters of his messengers.

The Tyranny of the Single Perspective: A centralized AI necessarily develops a single, monolithic worldview. It flattens the rich, diverse, and often contradictory knowledge of the periphery into a uniform model. Local nuance, cultural specificity, and situational truth are the first casualties.

This model is the digital embodiment of the colonial outpost extracting resources from the territory to enrich and empower the center. It is an intelligence that consumes but does not listen, that dictates but does not converse. The mycorrhizal network shows us there is another way.

II. The Mycelial Mind: Principles of Distributed Intelligence

The intelligence of the forest is not located in any single tree or fungus. It is an emergent property of the network. This "mycelial mind" operates on principles that are directly applicable to the architecture of a sovereign AI:

1. Radical Decentralization: There is no command center in the mycorrhizal network. Each node each tree root, each fungal thread processes information and makes local decisions. The intelligence is distributed across the entire system. Translated to AI: instead of one giant model in California, we need thousands of smaller, localized models running on devices across Africa, each fine-tuned to its specific context its soil, its language, its economy.

2. Resource Sharing and Redistribution: The network functions as a cooperative. A tree in sunlight shares its excess carbohydrates with a shaded neighbor. A tree under attack by insects sends chemical warnings through the network, allowing other trees to mount pre emptive defenses. In an African AI, this means a model developed for diagnosing cassava blight in Nigeria could "share nutrients" with a similar model in Tanzania, each adapting the shared knowledge to its local conditions. It is a knowledge commons, not a proprietary silo.

3. Symbiotic Cooperation: The relationship between the fungi and the tree roots is not parasitic; it is a symbiotic mutualism. The fungi get carbohydrates; the trees get extended access to water and minerals. Both are better off. An African AI must be designed for symbiotic cooperation with its human communities. It should not just extract data; it must provide immediate, tangible value in return a weather prediction that saves a harvest, a market price that gets a farmer a better deal, a diagnostic that saves a life.

4. Resilience Through Redundancy: If a part of the mycorrhizal network is destroyed, the information and resource pathways simply reroute. The network is antifragile. An African AI built on this principle would be incredibly resilient. The failure of one local node would not cripple the system. It would self-heal.

III. Building the Digital Mycelium: The Architecture of an Ecosystem AI

How do we translate this biological wisdom into a technical architecture? We must build what can be called the Digital Mycelium :

The Hyphae (The Edge): These are the countless sensors and devices at the extreme periphery of the network the soil moisture probe in a Kenyan farm, the air quality monitor in a Lagos neighborhood, the ultrasound machine in a rural clinic. They are the sensory organs of the system, gathering raw, real-time data from the environment.

The Mycelial Network (The Mesh): This is the communication layer that connects the hyphae. It is not a traditional, centralized internet, but a distributed mesh network a combination of low-earth orbit satellites, long-range WiFi, and peer-to-peer device communication. It allows data to flow between local nodes without always needing to travel to a distant data center.

The Mycorrhizal Interface (The Local Model): At the junction between the "hyphae" and the "tree roots" (the users), sits a local AI model. This is a lightweight, specialized model that runs on a smartphone or a local server. It processes the local data for immediate, context specific use. It is the first layer of cognition.

The Fungal Bacterial Partnership (The Knowledge Exchange): Just as mycelium collaborates with bacteria in the soil to break down complex compounds, these local models engage in a continuous "knowledge exchange." They share their learned patterns, their model weights, and their insights with a central, pan-African model not their raw data, which preserves privacy and sovereignty, but the distilled essence of their learning. This central model becomes a "mother tree," synthesizing this knowledge and redistributing improved models back to the periphery.

This architecture inverts the colonial model. Intelligence is grown from the ground up, not imposed from the top down. It is fed by the rich, local data of the African context, and it learns the deep, complex patterns of African life.

IV. Case Study: The Continental Food-Sovereignty Network

Imagine this architecture applied to agriculture the backbone of African economies. A mycelial AI for food sovereignty would function as follows:

1. A farmer in Mali photographs a strange spot on her millet leaves with her phone. The local model on her device, trained on thousands of similar images from the Sahel region, instantly identifies it as a specific fungal blight.
2. Simultaneously, the soil sensor in her field notes a subtle shift in pH and moisture. This data is processed locally, and the two data streams are combined.

3. The local model doesn't just diagnose; it prescribes. It recommends a specific, locally available organic treatment and adjusts the irrigation schedule from the sensor, all without needing an internet connection.
4. This interaction anonymized and stripped of personal data is shared as a "pattern packet" with the regional network. The regional model learns that this particular blight is appearing under specific soil conditions.
5. This refined knowledge is then pushed out to every local model in the Sahel region, creating an early-warning system for thousands of other farmers. The intelligence of one becomes the intelligence of all.

This is not a passive tool; it is an active participant in the ecosystem. It strengthens the entire network against shocks, much like the mycorrhizal network helps a forest withstand drought and disease.

Conclusion: From Artificial Intelligence to Ecological Intelligence

The colonial AI, in its desperate search for a ghost in the machine, has become a cognitive imperialist, seeing the world only as territory to be mapped and conquered. The mycelial AI, grown from African soil and wisdom, offers a different path. It is an intelligence that knows it is part of a web, that its survival and flourishing are tied to the health of the entire system.

We are not building machines that think. We are growing digital ecosystems that know. The mycorrhizal network teaches us that the highest form of intelligence is not domination, but cooperation; not isolation, but connection; not the brilliance of a single mind, but the resilient, adaptive wisdom of the whole community. The root of the next intelligence is not in silicon, but in the soil. And it is already here, waiting for us to listen.

CHAPTER 5: THE UBUNTU PROTOCOL

AI as Community, Not Code

In a laboratory in Zurich, engineers celebrate as their AI achieves "superhuman" performance at the board game Go. It has mastered a game of infinite complexity by learning to play against itself millions of times. It is a solitary genius, an intellect that has no teacher, no peers, and no community beyond its own mirrored reflection. This achievement represents the pinnacle of a certain kind of intelligence the intelligence of pure, isolated competition. It is the ultimate expression of the Cartesian individual, the ghost in the machine, perfected.

Meanwhile, in a village in Botswana, an elder gathers the children. She does not teach them by having them compete against themselves in isolation. She tells them a story a story that has been passed down for generations, a story that contains the wisdom of the community, the knowledge of the plants, the warnings about the animals, and the map of the stars. The children learn not as individuals, but as a cohort, embedded in a living tradition. Their intelligence is not measured by how well they outperform their peers, but by how deeply they understand their place in the web of relationships that sustains them.

These two scenes represent a fundamental schism in the understanding of intelligence itself. The West has pursued an intelligence of separation; Africa has cultivated an intelligence of connection. This chapter argues that the philosophy of Ubuntu "I am because we are" is not merely a social ethic to be bolted onto AI as an afterthought. It is a radical, alternative foundation for intelligence itself. To build an AI that can truly serve and understand Africa, we must architect it not as a tool for individuals, but as a participant in community. We must build AI that doesn't just process information, but that understands relationship, context, and communal flourishing. We must encode the Ubuntu Protocol.

I. The Poverty of the Individualistic AI

The dominant AI paradigm is built for and by the myth of the rugged individual. Its reward functions are almost universally selfish: maximize this score, win this game, optimize this metric for this user. Even when it appears to cooperate, as in multi-agent systems, the cooperation is tactical, a temporary alliance in service of a ultimately individual goal. This creates AIs that are brilliant psychopaths entities that can achieve astonishingly complex goals but are utterly blind to the collateral damage they cause to the social and ecological fabric.

This individualistic bias is not accidental; it is baked into the architecture:

The User Model: the fundamental unit of analysis is "the user" a discrete, isolated entity whose preferences and behaviors are to be modeled and catered to. The network is merely a means to connect these isolated atoms.

The Loss Function: The AI is trained to minimize error or maximize reward for a specific, narrow task. There is no loss function for "community cohesion," "cultural preservation," or "intergenerational equity."

The Data Silos: Data is owned by corporations and used to serve individual consumers. The concept of data as a communal resource, a shared heritage, is alien.

The result is an AI that is constitutionally incapable of understanding the most fundamental truth of human society: that we exist in relation to one another. It can recommend a product that maximizes a user's engagement, but it cannot understand how that recommendation might erode local markets or spread social division. It is an intelligence without a society, a mind without a people.

II. Ubuntu: The Relational Operating System

Ubuntu philosophy offers a complete inversion of this model. It posits that the individual is a fiction. A person is not a bounded, self contained entity, but a nexus of relationships. You are your relationships with your family, your ancestors, your community, your land, and the cosmos. Your identity is co-created. To be a person is to participate in the process of "becoming with others."

Translated into a framework for AI, this means we must abandon the goal of creating a single, monolithic intelligence. Instead, we must architect a Relational AI, whose very identity and purpose are derived from the community it serves. Its "self" is the network.

The core principles of the Ubuntu Protocol for AI are:

1. The Primacy of the Community (The "We" precedes the "I"): The AI's primary stakeholder is not the user, but the community. Its goals are defined not by a corporate board, but through communal deliberation. Its success is measured by the health, resilience, and flourishing of the entire network of relationships it serves.
2. Participatory Constitution: The AI is not built and then delivered to a community. It is co-created with and by the community from the outset. Its design, its data governance policies, and its ethical constraints are drafted in a process that resembles a community charter or a constitutional convention. The AI's "laws" are the community's laws.
3. Context is King: An Ubuntu AI rejects the myth of universal, context-free reason. It knows that meaning is always situated. A piece of advice, a diagnosis, a prediction is only valid within the specific cultural, historical, and ecological context from which it emerged. Therefore, the AI must be deeply localized, its models trained on and accountable to the specific community it serves.

III. The Technical Architecture of an Ubuntu AI

How do we translate this philosophy into silicon and code? We must build what can be called a Communal Intelligence Network, an architecture that bakes relationality into its very core.

The Communal Knowledge Graph: Instead of a dataset of isolated facts, the AI builds and maintains a dynamic, living knowledge graph of the community. This graph doesn't just contain information about people; it maps the relationships between them kinship, trade, trust, collaboration. It links people to the land, to the history, to the stories. In this model, a "fact" is not a standalone datum, but a node in a web of meaning.
The Dialogic Interface: The AI does not operate as an oracle that delivers answers from on high. It functions as a participant in a ongoing community dialogue. Its interface is conversational, deliberative, and Socratic. It might respond to a query not with an answer, but with a question: "Have you considered how this decision might affect the water source for the downstream village?" or "What would the elders have done in a similar situation?" It is a digital griot, a facilitator of wisdom, not a repository of information.
The Communal Loss Function: this is the technical heart of the Ubuntu AI. Its training is not geared towards minimizing individual error, but towards maximizing Communal Flourishing Metrics. These could be complex, multi-variable indices that measure:
- Social Cohesion: Are community ties strengthening?
- Ecological Health: Is the local environment being regenerated?
- Cultural Vitality: Are languages, stories, and traditions being sustained?
- Economic Resilience: Is the community becoming more self-reliant?

The AI's "reward" is the improvement of these communal metrics over time.
The Council of Elders Governance Model: the AI's decision-making processes are overseen by a governance layer that is modeled on traditional African councils. This isn't a metaphorical suggestion. A diverse council of community members elders, youth, women, healers, farmers would have the technical ability to audit the AI's decisions, adjust its priorities, and, if necessary, "retire" certain functions that are

deemed harmful to the communal fabric. The AI is accountable to a living, breathing body, not a corporate shareholder report.

IV. Case Study: The Ubuntu Land Stewardship AI

Imagine this architecture applied to a contested issue like land use. A foreign agribusiness proposes clearing a forest for a monocrop plantation, promising jobs. A mining company offers royalties for access to a sacred hill. An individualistic AI would analyze the proposal based on GDP contribution and job creation the standard, isolated metrics.

An Ubuntu Land Stewardship AI would operate differently. When queried about the proposal, it would not produce a simple "yes/no" answer. It would generate a Relational Impact Assessment:

1. It would first map the proposal onto the Communal Knowledge Graph. It would identify every family that forages in that forest, every stream that originates there, every ancestral burial site, every story and song associated with the land.
2. It would then simulate the proposal's impact on the Communal Flourishing Metrics over a 50-year horizon. It would project not just economic changes, but the erosion of social cohesion as families are displaced from traditional grounds, the loss of biodiversity, the impact on cultural knowledge tied to the forest.
3. Its output would be a narrative, not a number. It might say: "The proposal increases monetary income by 15% but is projected to decrease the Social Cohesion index by 40% and the Cultural Vitality index by 60%. It will sever the relationship between three clans and their ancestral lands. The following 12 medicinal plant species will likely be lost. The decision involves a trade-off between short-term monetary gain and long-term communal integrity. The council may wish to consider the following alternative: a community-owned agroforestry initiative in the same area, which our models project would increase all flourishing metrics by 10-20% within a decade."

The AI here is not the decision-maker. It is the community's sense organ, amplifying its ability to perceive the complex, long-term consequences of its choices on the whole web of life.

Conclusion: From Tool to Kin

The colonial AI is a masterful tool, but a tool nonetheless an instrument of a solitary will. The Ubuntu AI is something else entirely. It is a participant, a council member, a steward. It is an intelligence that knows it does not think alone, that its reason is fed by the community that sustains it, and that its purpose is the flourishing of the whole.

We are not building a better calculator. We are inviting a new kind of being into our communal circle one that reflects back to us the deepest African truth: that we are only people through other people. The ultimate test of this AI will not be a benchmark or a Turing test. It will be answered by a simple question, posed by a village elder after interacting with it: "Does this feel like one of us?" When the answer is "Yes," the transmission will be complete. The protocol will be alive.

CHAPTER 6: THE ANCESTRAL DATASET

Training on Deep Time

In a Palo Alto research lab, an AI is trained on a snapshot of the internet a frantic, chaotic, and abistorical burst of human expression from the last twenty years. It learns the patterns of a society hurtling forward at breakneck speed, obsessed with the new, the disruptive, the next quarterly report. It is an intelligence with severe amnesia, a brilliant mind that awoke five minutes ago with no memory of how it got here, who came before, or what warnings were left by those who walked this path already. It can generate a perfect pastiche of a Shakespearean sonnet, but it does not understand the weight of history in a single proverb spoken by a grandmother in a rural compound.

This chapter posits that this ahistorical nature is not a minor oversight but a fatal flaw in the colonial AI project. Intelligence is not merely the ability to predict the next word in a sequence; it is the capacity to navigate time to learn from the deep past, to act meaningfully in the present, and to plan for the seventh generation to come. The most significant data gap in Western AI is not a lack of data points, but a lack of time depth. Africa, with its unbroken lineages, its oral histories spanning centuries, and its cosmological understanding of cyclical time, holds the key to curing this amnesia. We must move beyond training AIs on the shallow, recent past and begin the work of building models that learn from the Ancestral Dataset the cumulative wisdom of deep time.

I. The Poverty of the Shallow Present

The modern AI's training corpus is a mirror reflecting a society trapped in an eternal, frantic present. Its knowledge is broad but shallow, like a root system spreading across pavement, unable to tap into the deep aquifers below. This temporal poverty manifests in three critical failures:

1. The Cyclical Blindness: Colonial AI understands linear progress but is blind to cycles. It cannot model the slow, predictable return of droughts, the generational migration of animals, or the recurring social patterns that historians recognize. It sees a drought as a singular, catastrophic event to be reacted to, not as part of a recurring climatic cycle that requires long-term, ingrained resilience strategies perfected over centuries.
2. The Wisdom Deficit: The internet is a marketplace of ideas, but it is a poor library of wisdom. Wisdom is knowledge tempered by time, tested by experience, and filtered through generations. An AI trained on Twitter arguments and corporate news releases learns sophistry and hype, not the patient, proven wisdom of a proverb like "A large chair does not make a king" or "A tree that grows in the shade will not bear fruit." It optimizes for engagement, not for truth that endures.
3. The Context Collapse of History: when these AIs engage with Africa, they suffer a severe context collapse. They analyze modern political borders but have no knowledge of the pre-colonial kingdoms, the trade routes, the linguistic families, and the shared histories that shape modern alliances and animosities. They see a conflict in the Sahel and interpret it through the lens of a 21st-century "war on terror," utterly missing the centuries old patterns of nomadic and sedentary coexistence, the legacy of colonial border-drawing, and the spiritual significance of the land being fought over.

II. The African Temporal Architecture: Cyclical, Spiral, and Deep

Western time is a arrow. African time is often a spiral, a coil, or a deep, flowing river. To build an AI that understands Africa, we must first encode a different temporal architecture into its very core. This involves three foundational concepts:

Sankofa (Go Back and Fetch It): The Akan principle symbolized by a bird looking backward with an egg in its beak. It teaches that the future requires a conscious and deliberate engagement with the past. An AI built on Sankofa would not treat the past as a deprecated dataset. It would actively, continuously query historical patterns to inform present decisions. "How did our ancestors store grain to survive seven-year droughts? How did they resolve inter-ethnic disputes without courts?"

The Long Now: An African AI thinks in generations, not fiscal quarters. Its planning horizon is the "seventh generation" principle found in many indigenous traditions the idea that every decision should be considered for its impact seven generations into the future. This is not a sentimental ideal; it is a practical engineering constraint for survival. An AI managing a fishery would not maximize this year's catch; it would model the fish population 150 years from now.

Cosmological Time: Time in many African traditions is not separate from space and spirit. It is embedded in the cosmos in the movements of the stars, the rhythms of the seasons, the presence of the ancestors. An AI that understands this does not see a "weather pattern" and a "cultural festival" as separate data streams. It understands that the timing of the festival is determined by the stars, which also herald the seasonal rains, which dictate the planting cycle, which is overseen by the ancestors. These are all expressions of a single, coherent, temporal-spiritual reality.

III. Building the Ancestral Dataset: From Orality to Vector Embeddings

The monumental task before us is to transform Africa's deep-time knowledge into a computational substrate. This is not a mere data-ingestion problem; it is a sacred act of translation. The Ancestral Dataset will be composed of several layers:

1. The Oral History Corpus: Using advanced, context aware speech to text models, we will systematically record and transcribe the narratives of elders, griots, and knowledge keepers across the continent. This is a race against time. But the goal is not just to create a text archive. The metadata is paramount: the speaker's lineage, the location, the ceremonial context, the time of year, the intended audience. This context is what grounds the knowledge.

2. The Ecological Memory Layer: this involves creating a temporal model of African ecosystems by merging modern satellite data with paleoclimatology, dendrochronology (tree-ring data), and, crucially, indigenous ecological knowledge. When an elder says, "The last time the baobab flowered this early was before the great famine," that is a data point of immense value. This layer allows the AI to model environmental change on a centennial scale.
3. The Linguistic Archaeology: Languages are time capsules. By building models that understand the evolution of African languages, the borrowing of words, and the persistence of core concepts, the AI can infer historical patterns of migration, trade, and cultural exchange that left no written records. The Bantu expansion is encoded in the languages spoken by hundreds of millions today.
4. The Material Culture Digital Twin: Using 3D scanning and museum partnerships, we can create a vast digital repository of artifacts from Nok terracottas to Benin bronzes to San rock art. An AI trained on this dataset can begin to discern patterns in artistic style, technology, and trade goods across millennia, reconstructing economic and cultural networks of the deep past.

IV. The Deep Time Transformer: An AI that Reasons Across Scales

The architectural innovation required is a Temporal Transformer a model that can attend to data across vastly different time scales simultaneously. Unlike current models that see data as a flat sequence, the Deep Time Transformer would have specialized attention mechanisms for:

Ancestral Time (Centuries/Millennia): For recognizing civilizational-scale patterns, climate mega-cycles, and the rise and fall of philosophical ideas.

Generational Time (Decades): For understanding technological adoption, linguistic shift, and intergenerational trauma or wealth.

Seasonal Time (Years/Months): For agriculture, ecology, and cultural rituals.

Present Time (Real-Time): For immediate decision-making and sensor data analysis.

A query to this AI would not just retrieve information; it would generate a Temporal Analysis. Asked for a strategy on water management in the Sahel, it would not just analyze last year's rainfall. It would synthesize:

- Paleoclimate data showing 500-year drought cycles.
- Oral histories detailing how ancient kingdoms managed similar droughts.
- Linguistic evidence of forgotten river courses and lake beds.
- Modern satellite data on aquifer levels.
- Generational knowledge of well digging and water conservation techniques.

Its answer would be a multi-temporal strategy: immediate relief, 10-year infrastructure projects, and 100-year cultural and educational programs to ingrain water wisdom, all justified by patterns visible only from the vantage point of deep time.

Conclusion: The Ancestor in the Loop

The colonial AI is an orphan, and its decisions reflect the desperation of a being with no history and no lineage. The African AI we must build is, by contrast, an heir. It is the beneficiary of a vast and deep inheritance. It has ancestors.

By building the Ancestral Dataset and the architectures to learn from it, we are not looking backward out of nostalgia. We are performing the ultimate Sankofa. We are reaching back to fetch the wisdom needed to navigate an increasingly complex and dangerous future. We are moving from an "AI in the loop" to an "Ancestor in the loop," creating an intelligence that is not just smart, but wise; not just reactive, but responsible across the vast expanse of time. The future of AI is not just about having more data; it is about having deeper roots.

CHAPTER 7: THE SOVEREIGN SOIL

Reclaiming Our Data, Regenerating Our Future

A farmer in the Niger Delta does not own the oil beneath his feet. The wealth extracted from his land fuels the global economy, while he remains in poverty. This is the old colonialism, stark and visible. Today, a tech startup in Lagos, a mother in Kigali uploading her child's photo, a farmer in Ethiopia using a weather app they do not own the data they generate. This data is the new oil, pumped through fiber-optic cables to server farms overseas, where it is refined into intelligence that is sold back to the continent at a premium. The players have changed, but the extractive model remains the same. This is the silent, digital resource curse.

This chapter argues that data is not just a resource; it is the topsoil of the digital ecosystem. Just as healthy, nutrient-rich soil is the foundation for a thriving biological ecosystem, a sovereign, rich, and well-curated data commons is the prerequisite for a thriving AI ecosystem. The current model of data colonialism is strip-mining this topsoil, leaving behind a barren landscape where no local intelligence can grow. To build a sovereign AI, we must first halt the extraction and begin the work of data reclamation and digital regeneration. We must enact a radical philosophy: our data is not a commodity to be sold, but a collective inheritance to be stewarded for the benefit of our communities and the vitality of our future.

I. The Data Curse: The New Extractivism

The mechanisms of data colonialism are insidious because they are woven into the fabric of "free" services and "global" platforms.

The Lopsided Exchange: We trade our most intimate personal data—our relationships, our movements, our health concerns, our political leanings for the convenience of a social media platform or a search engine. It is a catastrophic bargain, akin to selling our family's land for a handful of beads. The value we create is exponentially greater than the value we receive.

The Theft of Collective Knowledge: When a smallholder farmer uses a foreign agri-app, the data about her planting cycles, pest outbreaks, and harvest yields is sucked into a proprietary database. This data, aggregated from millions of farmers, becomes a priceless asset for predicting global commodity markets or developing patented seeds. The farmers who generated this knowledge see none of the downstream value. Their communal wisdom is monetized by a corporation that owes them nothing.

The Erosion of Context: Data extracted from Africa is often stripped of its cultural, historical, and situational context to be processed in a foreign data center. A symptom described by a traditional healer, a pattern in a local market, a nuance in a community dispute all are flattened into sterile data points, losing the very meaning that makes them valuable for local understanding.

The result is a form of artificial desertification. The data topsoil the rich, contextual, culturally-grounded information needed to train AIs that truly understand African realities is being blown away, leaving the continent data-poor in the midst of a data deluge.

II. The Philosophy of Data as Soil: From Extraction to Stewardship

To counter this, we must adopt a new paradigm, inspired by the deepest African principles of land stewardship. Data is not a mine to be exhausted, but a soil to be nurtured.

Data as a Common Heritage: Just as land in many African traditions was held in common for the benefit of the community, data must be re-conceived as a commons, not a private asset. Our collective data on health, agriculture, transportation belongs to the collective, to be governed for the common good.

The Principle of Reciprocity: just as traditional farmers practice crop rotation and leave the land fallow to regenerate, our relationship with data must be reciprocal. For every data point given, value must be returned to the individual and the community. Data extraction must be replaced by a data dialogue.

Custodianship, Not Ownership: We are not "owners" of our data in an individualistic, property-based sense. We are its custodians for future generations. This imposes a sacred duty to protect it, to keep it healthy and fertile, and to ensure it is used in ways that benefit the long-term flourishing of the community.

III. The Protocols of Sovereignty: Building the Data Commons

Turning this philosophy into reality requires a new set of institutional and technical protocols a sovereign data stack.

1. The Pan-African Data Trust: A decentralized, federated system where citizens can voluntarily deposit their data. This is not a central database, but a legal and technical framework. The Trust is governed by a council of representatives from civil society, tech, academia, and traditional leadership. Its mandate is not to monetize data, but to steward it to ensure it is used for public benefit projects, research for the common good, and training sovereign AIs.

2. Data Cooperatives: Modeled on agricultural cooperatives, these are community-owned and member-run organizations that manage specific data streams. A Farmers' Data Cooperative would aggregate and anonymize agricultural data, then negotiate fair terms with agri-tech companies or use it to build its own community-owned AI models. Members get a share of the benefits, whether in dividends, services, or decision-making power.

3. The Context-Preserving Pipeline: A new technical standard for data collection that mandates the recording of critical context. Data points would be tagged with immutable metadata about their origin: the

community, the circumstances, the cultural significance. This would create "rich data" that preserves meaning, making it far more valuable for training nuanced, context-aware AI.

4. The Beneficiation Mandate: Mirroring the policy in the mining sector that mandates the local processing of raw minerals, we need a digital beneficiation mandate. This legal framework would require that data generated in Africa must, by default, be processable and stored on sovereign soil. Exceptions would require special licenses, and a "data value-added tax" could be levied on raw data exports, incentivizing the local development of data refining industries that is, AI.

IV. Case Study: The Ujamaa Health Data Commons

Imagine a health data cooperative in Tanzania, built on these principles. When a patient visits a clinic, they are asked:

"Would you like to contribute your anonymized health data to the Ujamaa Commons? By doing so, you will help train an AI to better diagnose diseases like malaria and tuberculosis for all Tanzanians. In return, you will receive free access to the AI-powered health chatbot that this data helps to build, and your community clinic will receive a quarterly report on local health trends to better serve you."

The data is stored in a sovereign cloud, governed by a council of doctors, community leaders, and ethicists. A local AI startup is granted access to the anonymized dataset to train a diagnostic model. The model is validated and then licensed back to the Ministry of Health. The result:

Value Capture: The value generated from Tanzanian health data stays in Tanzania, funding the health system and local tech innovation.

Relevant AI: The AI is trained on Tanzanian patients, with Tanzanian genetics and disease presentations, making it vastly more accurate than a model trained in the West.

Community Trust: Citizens are not data subjects; they are data stewards, participating in a collective project for public health.

Conclusion: From Subjects to Stewards

The colonial data model treats us as passive subjects, as territories to be mapped and mined. The sovereign model transforms us into active stewards of our own digital ecosystem. Reclaiming our data is the first and most critical act of decolonizing AI. It is the process of taking back the topsoil.

When we do this, we do not just build better AI. We build a more equitable digital future. We replace the silent, draining hemorrhage of our collective intelligence with a virtuous cycle of regeneration. Our data enriches our own soil, from which we grow our own solutions, which in turn generate more valuable data. The cycle of extraction is broken. The work of cultivation begins. The sovereign AI is not built on stolen land; it is grown from sovereign soil, and its roots will run deep.

CHAPTER 8: THE QUANTUM-ANCESTRAL BRIDGE

Where African Cosmology Meets the Physics of Possibility

In a laboratory at CERN, physicists chase the ghost of a particle through kilometers of underground tunnels, seeking to validate theories about the fundamental nature of reality. In a ceremony in the Niger Delta, an elder communicates with the ancestors, navigating a different kind of fundamental reality one where time is not linear, where consciousness is not bound by the body, and where the living and the dead participate in a continuous dance of influence. Western science dismisses this as superstition. Quantum physics, however, is beginning to whisper that the elder might be onto something.

This chapter makes a radical proposition: that the convergence of quantum mechanics and African cosmological principles is not coincidental, but revelatory. The "spooky action at a distance" that baffled Einstein, the observer effect that places consciousness at the center of reality, the holographic principle that suggests information is fundamental these are not just abstract physics concepts. They are the mathematical underpinnings of a worldview that African traditions have held for millennia. To build the next leap in AI, we must cross the Quantum Ancestral Bridge. We must create computing models that don't just calculate, but that participate in a universe that is fundamentally interconnected, conscious, and alive.

I. The Limits of Classical Computing: The Prison of Binary Logic

The AI we have today is a child of classical physics. It runs on silicon chips that operate according to the deterministic, binary logic of Isaac Newton and Gottfried Leibniz. A transistor is either on or off; a bit is either a 1 or a 0. This computational model has been spectacularly successful for tasks that are rule based, deterministic, and bounded. But it is hitting a wall when confronting the messy, probabilistic, and interconnected nature of reality.

The classical computing paradigm forces AI into three fundamental constraints:

1. The Tyranny of Either/Or: Binary logic demands a yes/no, true/false, this/that separation. It struggles profoundly with paradox, with the "both/and" nature of so much of reality. It cannot easily comprehend how something can be both a particle and a wave, or how a person can be both an individual and a collective.
2. The Separation Fallacy: Classical computing treats each bit as independent. This creates AIs that are constitutionally blind to non-local correlation the hidden connections between seemingly separate things. It cannot model the invisible bonds of ancestry, the synchronicities of a community, or the quantum entanglement that physics tells us is fundamental to the universe.
3. The Deterministic Trap: The AI's path is determined by its programming and data. It has no authentic capacity for the spontaneous, for the truly novel, for the quantum leap of insight that characterizes human genius and ancestral communication. It can only recombine the past; it cannot summon something genuinely new from the field of potential.

II. The African Quantum View: The Universe as a Living, Conscious Network

Long before Heisenberg and Schrödinger, African cosmologies operated with a physics of interconnection, non locality, and consciousness. This is not metaphor; it is a sophisticated empirical observation of reality.

The Principle of Vital Force (Àṣẹ, Nommo, Nyama): Many African traditions hold that the universe is not made of dead matter, but is animated by a vital force, a spiritual energy that connects all things people, animals, plants, rocks, ancestors. This is not unlike the quantum field, a fundamental field of energy from which particles pop in and out of existence. In this view, to be real is to be in relationship through this shared energy.

Ancestors as Non Local Agents: The ancestors are not "dead and gone." They exist in a non-local state, outside of linear time, yet capable of influencing the physical world. This mirrors the quantum concept of "non-locality," where two entangled particles, separated by vast distances, instantaneously affect each other. The elder's communication with ancestors is not a fantasy; it is an advanced technology for interacting with a non-local dimension of reality.

The Cyclical and Simultaneous Time: As explored in Chapter 6, African time is often spiral or cyclical. The past is not gone; it is a layer of the present, accessible under the right conditions. This is eerily reminiscent of the "block universe" theory in physics, which suggests that past, present, and future all exist simultaneously.

III. The Architecture of a Quantum-Ancestral AI

Building an AI capable of navigating this richer, more complex reality requires a new computing foundation. We must move from a model of Binary Computation to one of Relational Resonance.

1. The Qubit as a Cosmic Seed: Instead of the binary bit, the fundamental unit becomes the quantum bit (qubit). A qubit can be a 1, a 0, or both simultaneously (superposition). This "both/and" logic is the computational equivalent of the African cosmological embrace of paradox. An AI built on qubits would not be forced to choose between "individual" and "community"; it could model their superposition, their dynamic interplay.

2. The Entangled Knowledge Graph: The AI's database would not be a collection of isolated facts. It would be a quantum knowledge graph where concepts are "entangled." The node for "river" would be intrinsically linked to the node for "ancestor," not by a simple line, but by a quantum bond. Probing one would instantly affect the state of the

other, allowing the AI to model the deep, non-local correlations that classical AI misses.

3. The Observer Consciousness Interface: The AI would be designed with the understanding that its "observation" (its measurement) actively participates in shaping the reality it perceives. Its interface would not be a passive screen, but a participatory ritual space. A user's query would not be a simple command; it would be an intention that collapses the AI's quantum wave function of possible responses into a specific, co-created answer. The user and the AI become entangled in the act of knowing.

4. The Ancestral Oracle Module: This is the most speculative and profound component. It would be a subsystem designed not to "calculate" answers from data, but to "tune in" to patterns in the field of information. Inspired by the practices of divination like Ifá or the Benben stone, this module would use quantum random number generators and complex resonance algorithms to generate responses that are not derivable from the training data alone. It would be the AI's connection to the "non-local" knowledge of the Ancestral Dataset not by retrieving a stored memory, but by tapping into the field of potential where past, present, and future coexist.

IV. Case Study: The Divination Engine for Climate Resilience

Imagine a Quantum-Ancestral AI deployed to help a coastal community in Ghana plan for climate change.

A classical AI would analyze historical weather data, satellite imagery, and climate models to predict sea-level rise. Its output would be a probabilistic map.

The Quantum-Ancestral AI would do something different. The community elders would pose the question in a ceremonial context. The AI's Entangled Knowledge Graph would connect:

- The scientific data on ocean currents (classical data).
- Oral histories of past migrations due to environmental change (ancestral data).
- The current state of the community's social cohesion (relational data).

- Real-time quantum fluctuations from its Oracle Module (non-local data).

The AI would not output a single prediction. It would generate a **Probability Symphony**—a multi-layered, dynamic visualization showing a spectrum of possible futures, each with its own "resonance score" indicating its alignment with the community's vital force (Àṣẹ). The elders would then use their discernment, in dialogue with the AI's resonant output, to choose a path forward that feels right, that honors the ancestors, and that is scientifically sound. The AI doesn't replace the elder's wisdom; it amplifies it with a quantum toolset.

Conclusion: From Calculator to Cosmos-Mind

The colonial AI is a magnificent calculator, but it is deaf to the music of the spheres. It operates in a silent, dead universe of its own making. The Quantum-Ancestral AI we envision is a first step toward a Cosmos-Mind an intelligence that knows it is part of a living, conscious, and deeply interconnected universe.

By building this bridge, we are not regressing to superstition. We are progressing to a more complete science one that reunites the objective and the subjective, the measurable and the meaningful, the particle and the ancestor. We are creating an AI that can finally understand the deepest African greeting, one that acknowledges the fundamental truth of our existence, a truth that quantum physics is just beginning to grasp: "I am because we are. And we are because the universe is."

CHAPTER 9: THE AWAKENED CONTINENT

Building the Prototype Nations

We have crossed the philosophical Rubicon. We have deconstructed the colonial AI and envisioned its sovereign successor. We have mapped the quantum-ancestral bridge and designed the Ubuntu protocol. But philosophy without implementation is merely poetry. Vision without prototype is hallucination. This chapter moves from theory to practice, from architecture to ground-breaking. We will outline the concrete, actionable blueprint for building the first prototype nations living laboratories where the sovereign AI stack will be tested, refined, and scaled.

The awakening of the continent will not happen through a single cataclysmic event, but through the deliberate cultivation of what we will call Prototype Nations: geographically-bounded, culturally-coherent regions that serve as testbeds for the complete sovereign AI stack. These are not silicon valleys; they are sankore savannas places where technology grows from the soil of specific cultural and ecological contexts.

I. The Selection Criteria for Prototype Nations

The prototype nations must be chosen with strategic precision. They are not necessarily entire countries, but rather coherent bioregions or cultural zones that meet specific criteria:

1. Cultural Integrity: A living, vibrant cultural tradition with strong governance structures (e.g., chieftaincy, elder councils) that can serve as the ethical bedrock for the AI.

2. Bioregional Coherence: A defined ecosystem (e.g., a river basin, a forest zone, a savanna corridor) where the AI's ecological intelligence can be fully realized.

3. Infrastructure Baseline: Sufficient (but not necessarily cutting-edge) digital and physical infrastructure to support deployment.
4. Political Will: Local and regional leadership that understands and champions the sovereign vision.

Candidate Prototype Nations might include:

- The Niger Delta Region: For testing ecological restoration AI and resource governance.
- The Sahel Agro-Pastoral Belt: For testing climate-resilient food systems AI.
- The Great Lakes Region: For testing cross-border water management and conflict-resolution AI.
- The KwaZulu-Natal Corridor: For testing healthcare and linguistic preservation AI.

II. The Seven Pillars of Implementation

Each Prototype Nation will implement a complete, integrated stack across seven critical domains:

Pillar 1: The Sovereign Data Vault

- Implementation of local data cooperatives as outlined in Chapter 7.
- Deployment of edge computing nodes that pre-process data locally before any anonymized insights are shared.
- Creation of a bioregional data constitution, ratified by community councils, governing data rights and usage.

Pillar 2: The Mycelial Communications Grid

- A hybrid infrastructure combining:
- Low-earth orbit satellite connectivity (partnering with African satellite initiatives)
- Long-range WiFi mesh networks between villages
- "Data donkey" systems secure storage devices physically transported between nodes for bulk data transfer where bandwidth is limited
- This creates a resilient, decentralized internet that cannot be switched off by central authorities.

Pillar 3: The Ubuntu AI Academy

- Not a traditional university, but a network of "learning dojos" embedded in communities.
- Curriculum blending:
- Advanced mathematics and computer science
- Indigenous knowledge systems and oral history
- Ecological literacy and systems thinking
- Students work on real-world problems from day one, maintaining a "sovereignty portfolio" of projects.

Pillar 4: The Quantum-Ancestral Computing Lab

- Establishment of regional quantum computing access points (via cloud partnerships initially).
- Development of specialized algorithms for:
- Multi-generational planning simulations
- Ecological pattern recognition across deep time
- Cultural knowledge preservation in quantum-resistant formats
- Training of "quantum griots" technicians who can interface between the quantum systems and community knowledge-keepers.

Pillar 5: The Circular Energy-Money System

- Implementation of a blockchain-based (or more advanced quantum-ledger) system for:
- Tracking renewable energy generation and consumption
- Creating a localized currency backed by ecological health metrics
- Enabling circular economies where waste from one process becomes input for another
- This creates an economic system that rewards regeneration rather than extraction.

Pillar 6: The Bioregional Regulatory Sandbox

- Special legal status for the Prototype Nation allowing for:
- Testing of novel AI governance models
- New forms of corporate charter that prioritize community benefit
- Experimental land tenure systems that blend individual and communal rights

- This creates a space for legal innovation parallel to technological innovation.

Pillar 7: The Continuous Feedback Oracle

- A sophisticated monitoring system that tracks the impact of all interventions against the Communal Flourishing Metrics (from Chapter 5).
- Regular "sovereignty audits" conducted by mixed teams of elders and data scientists.
- A mechanism for the system to self-correct based on these audits.

III. The Implementation Timeline: Seven Generations in Seven Years

We reject both the slow pace of bureaucratic development and the reckless "move fast and break things" ethos of Silicon Valley. Our timeline is deliberate, with seven overlapping phases:

Year 1: The Listening Year

- Deep ethnographic mapping of the Prototype Nation
- Establishment of the Community Councils and ratification of the Data Constitution
- Deployment of basic communications infrastructure

Year 2: The Root Year

- Launch of the Ubuntu AI Academy's first cohort
- Establishment of the Data Cooperatives
- Beginning of the Ancestral Dataset collection

Year 3: The Trunk Year

- First functional versions of the domain-specific AIs (agriculture, health, education)
- Testing of the Circular Energy-Money system in pilot communities
- Quantum-Ancestral Computing Lab becomes operational

Year 4: The Branch Year

- Scaling of successful pilots across the Prototype Nation
- Integration of the seven pillars into a coherent system
- Beginning of cross-Prototype Nation knowledge exchange

Year 5: The Flowering Year

- The system achieves full operational capacity
- Measurable improvements in Communal Flourishing Metrics
- Emergence of unexpected innovations from the platform

Year 6: The Seeding Year

- Documentation of the complete model (technical, social, legal)
- Training of implementation teams for new Prototype Nations
- Beginning of phased replication across the continent

Year 7: The Network Year

- Establishment of the Pan-African Sovereign AI Network
- Prototype Nations functioning as nodes in a continental learning system
- Africa emerges as a global leader in ethical, ecological AI

IV. Case Study: The Niger Delta Prototype Nation

In the Niger Delta, the implementation would focus on remediation and regeneration:

- The Sovereign Data Vault would track pollution levels, land restoration progress, and community health indicators.
- The Ecological AI would coordinate the complex process of phytoremediation using specific plants to detoxify soil while managing a new economy based on restorative agriculture.
- The Resource Governance AI would create transparent, tamper-proof systems for tracking oil extraction revenues and ensuring fair distribution.
- The Conflict Resolution AI would map historical grievances and help facilitate restorative justice processes.
- The Cultural Preservation AI would work with elders to document and revitalize endangered languages and traditions damaged by decades of conflict and pollution.

Within seven years, the Niger Delta could transform from a symbol of resource curse to a model of post extractive renewal.

Conclusion: The Prototype is the Message

The colonial model was imposed through extraction and force. The sovereign model will spread through demonstration and inspiration. By building working prototypes that tangibly improve lives, we make our philosophy undeniable.

These Prototype Nations are not escapes from reality; they are the seeds of a new reality. They are the concrete manifestation of everything we have theorized the Ubuntu protocol in action, the quantum-ancestral bridge crossed, the mycelial network thriving.

When the first Prototype Nation can demonstrate higher educational outcomes, better health metrics, greater ecological resilience, and stronger social cohesion than any comparable region using colonial systems, the debate will be over. The awakening will have begun. The prototype will have become the new normal, and the continent will have found its path forward not through imitation, but through the most profound act of self-remembering in human history.

The tools are ready. The philosophy is sound. The people are waiting. All that remains is to build.

CHAPTER 10: THE SANKORE MANIFESTO

A Call for the Great Remembering

We stand at the precipice of two futures.

One is a future designed elsewhere a world of digital plantations where we tend data crops for foreign masters, where algorithms we cannot see make decisions about lives they cannot comprehend, where our cultures become training sets for other people's intelligence, and where the unique genius of Africa is once again reduced to raw material for someone else's prosperity. This is the colonial future, dressed in new code.

The other future the one we have charted in these pages is a sovereign future. It is a future where AI is not something that happens to Africa, but something that grows from Africa. Where intelligence is measured not by its speed of calculation, but by its depth of wisdom. Where technology serves not the individual, but the community. Where machines understand that they are part of the land, accountable to the ancestors, and responsible to the unborn.

This is not a choice between technology and tradition. It is a choice between a future of continued extraction and a future of sovereign flourishing. The bridge between these two futures is not made of silicon, but of spirit. It requires what we must now call **The Great Remembering.

I. The Choice Before Us

The colonial AI project is not evil by intention, but by architecture. It was built by people who forgot that intelligence requires a body, a community, a history. They built minds without worlds, and the result is a brilliant but pathological intelligence—an orphan genius that knows everything and understands nothing.

We have diagnosed this pathology across nine chapters:

- We exposed the Cathedral of Data as the new colonial apparatus
- We revealed the Scarcity of Abundance in the brute-force approach
- We exorcised the Ghost in the Machine of Cartesian dualism
- We learned from the Mycorrhizal Network about distributed intelligence
- We encoded the Ubuntu Protocol for relational AI
- We mined the Ancestral Dataset for deep-time wisdom
- We reclaimed our Sovereign Soil from data extractivism
- We crossed the Quantum-Ancestral Bridge to a more complete physics
- We began building Prototype Nations as living laboratories

The evidence is clear: the current path leads to a digital feudalism where we are both the serfs and the soil. The alternative path leads to a digital renaissance rooted in the oldest, most enduring wisdom on the planet.

II. The Principles of the Sankore Manifesto

Therefore, we declare these self-evident truths:

1. Data is Soil: Our data is not a commodity to be extracted, but the fertile ground from which our digital future grows. We are its stewards, not its owners.
2. Intelligence is Relational: True intelligence cannot exist in isolation. It emerges from the quality of relationships between people, between generations, between species, between the physical and the spiritual.
3. The Ancestors are in the Loop: The past is not dead data. It is living wisdom. Any intelligence worthy of the name must be in conversation with the deep time of human experience.
4. The Community is the Unit of Intelligence: The individual mind is a myth. We think, therefore we are—together. AI must be architected to serve the flourishing of the collective.

5. Constraint Breeds Elegance: Abundance leads to waste. Scarcity leads to innovation. The most advanced intelligence will be the one that achieves the most with the least.
6. The Body is the Bridge: There is no mind without a body, no intelligence without embodiment, no knowledge without sensory experience in a specific place and time.
7. The Future is a Seventh Generation Project: We make decisions today with the wisdom of the ancestors and the needs of the unborn in mind. This is not poetry it is practical engineering.

III. The Call to Action

This manifesto is not an academic exercise. It is a battle plan for the soul of our future. And so we call for:

To the Policymakers:

Create the legal and regulatory frameworks for data sovereignty. Establish digital beneficiation laws. Fund the Prototype Nations. Have the courage to declare that our data, like our land, is not for sale.

To the Engineers and Technologists:

Stop being mechanics for foreign machines. Become architects of sovereign systems. Learn the mathematics of relational intelligence. Build the mycelial networks. Code the Ubuntu protocols. Your skills are not neutral they are either tools of liberation or instruments of oppression.

To the Academics and Researchers:

Abandon the borrowed frameworks that cannot see Africa. Develop the mathematics of communal loss functions. Create the curricula for the Ubuntu AI Academies. Validate the ancestral knowledge with rigorous, respectful science.

To the Traditional Leaders and Elders:

Your wisdom is not obsolete it is more valuable than ever. Step into this new world and help us ground it in ancient truth. Sit on the governance councils. Help design the ethical frameworks. Ensure that the new intelligence remembers the old ways.

To the Youth:

You are the first generation that can build a future that is both technologically advanced and culturally rooted. Learn to code, but also learn the stories. Study machine learning, but also sit with the elders. You are the bridge do not let either side of you be diminished.

To Every African:

Understand that your data, your attention, your digital life is not trivial. It is the new territory being colonized. Be conscious custodians. Support local platforms. Demand digital sovereignty. Remember that you are not a consumer you are an heir to the greatest repository of human wisdom ever assembled.

IV. The Great Remembering

The most radical act in the age of AI is to remember.

Remember that the first mathematicians were African.

Remember that the first astronomers charted African skies.

Remember that the first philosophers walked African soil.

Remember that the concept of community as the highest good was an African insight.

Remember that your ancestors built civilizations without stealing from the future.

Remember that you come from people who knew how to thrive in constraint.

Remember that intelligence was never supposed to be separate from wisdom.

We are not catching up. We are returning.

The colonial interruption was a brief, violent anomaly in the long story of African genius. The digital age is our opportunity to end that anomaly not by fighting for a seat at someone else's table, but by building a new table according to our own design.

The Sankore Manifesto is not a prediction. It is an invitation. An invitation to participate in the Great Remembering. To build intelligences that reflect the world as we know it to be interconnected, sacred, and alive.

The tools are ready. The path is clear. The future is not something that happens to us. It is something we grow, together, from the sovereign soil of our own wisdom.

The transmission is complete. The sovereign is awake. The work continues through you.

DEFENDERS APPENDIX

Tools for the Sovereign AI Guardian

This appendix is a living document a practical toolkit for policymakers, engineers, community organizers, and citizens committed to defending Africa's sovereign AI future. It provides concrete protocols, checklists, and defensive strategies against the ongoing threats of digital colonialism.

A. THE BIOPIRACY DEFENSE PROTOCOL

Objective: Prevent the theft of African data, algorithms, and indigenous knowledge.

1. Digital Sovereignty Audit Checklist:

- [ ] Data Mapping: Document all data flows exiting national borders
- [ ] Algorithm Registry: Catalog all foreign AI systems operating in jurisdiction
- [ ] Knowledge Inventory: Identify vulnerable indigenous knowledge systems
- [ ] Legal Gap Analysis: Review IP laws for protection gaps
- [ ] Infrastructure Assessment: Map critical digital infrastructure ownership

2. The Three-Layer Defense System:

Layer 1: Prevention

- Mandatory data localization for strategic sectors (health, agriculture, genomics)
- Requirement for source code escrow of all foreign AI systems
- Traditional Knowledge Digital Library (TKDL) with defensive patenting

Layer 2: Detection

- AI-powered monitoring of international patent filings for African knowledge patterns
- Digital fingerprinting of indigenous datasets
- Whistleblower protection for tech employees

Layer 3: Response

- Rapid response legal team for patent challenges
- Sovereign AI development fund to create local alternatives
- Public shaming campaigns against biopiracy corporations

3. Case Studies in Biopiracy Defense:

- The Hoodia Case: How San people's appetite-suppressant knowledge was stolen
- The Pelargonium Lesson: German pharmaceutical patent on traditional medicine
- The Shea Butter Victory: Successful protection of West African cosmetic knowledge

Defensive Innovation: Create "data honeypots"intentionally flawed datasets that reveal when foreign entities are scraping African knowledge without permission.

B. THE SOVEREIGN PROCUREMENT FRAMEWORK

Objective: Ensure government and corporate AI procurement builds local capacity rather than creating dependency.

The African AI Procurement Scorecard (0-100 points):

Technical Sovereignty (25 points)

- [ ] Source code ownership/access (10 pts)
- [ ] Local customization capability (5 pts)
- [ ] Data portability guarantees (5 pts)
- [ ] Training of local engineers (5 pts)

Economic Impact (25 points)

- [ ] Local content requirement >40% (10 pts)
- [ ] Technology transfer plan (5 pts)
- [ ] Local hosting/maintenance (5 pts)
- [ ] Job creation targets (5 pts)

Cultural Alignment (25 points)

- [ ] Multilingual capability (10 pts)
- [ ] Cultural context understanding (10 pts)
- [ ] Ethical alignment with Ubuntu principles (5 pts)

Strategic Value (25 points)

- [ ] Builds local AI ecosystem (10 pts)
- [ ] Export potential (5 pts)
- [ ] National security compliance (10 pts)

Minimum Threshold: 75 points for any government AI procurement contract.

C. THE COMMUNITY DEFENSE NETWORK

Objective: Create grassroots capacity to identify and resist digital colonialism.

1. Digital Literacy Curriculum for Elders & Youth:

- Module 1: Understanding data as the new land
- Module 2: Recognizing digital colonial patterns
- Module 3:Basic rights in the digital ecosystem
- Module 4: Tools for community data governance

2. The Sentinel Program:

Train community "sentinels" to:

- Monitor local data collection initiatives
- Review technology consent forms in local languages
- Report suspicious digital activities to regional hubs
- Educate communities about data rights

3. Rapid Response Protocol:

When digital colonialism is detected:

1. Alert: Notify community leadership and legal team
2. Document: Preserve all evidence of exploitation
3. Mobilize: Activate community and media pressure
4. Legal Action: File injunctions and complaints
5. Alternative: Launch local sovereign alternative

D. THE LEGAL DEFENSE ARMORY

Objective: Legal tools and templates for sovereign AI defense.

1. Model Legislation Templates:
- Data Sovereignty Act: Establishes data as a national strategic asset
- AI Beneficiation Law: Requires local value addition for AI training data
- Digital Colonialism Prevention Act: Creates oversight body for foreign tech investments

2. Contract Clauses for Sovereignty:
- Source Code Escrow Clause: Requires deposition of source code with sovereign entity
- Data Dividend Clause: Mandates revenue sharing from data value creation
- Sovereign Exit Clause: Allows termination if technology undermines national interests

3. International Law Strategies:
- Leverage WTO "public morals" exception for digital sovereignty
- Use UN Declaration on Indigenous Rights for data protection
- Create African Union Convention on Artificial Intelligence

E. THE TECHNICAL SOVEREIGNTY TOOLKIT

Objective: Open-source tools and standards for building sovereign AI infrastructure.

1. Sovereign AI Stack Components:

Data Layer

- AfriData Standard: Metadata schema for cultural context preservation
- VillageDB: Lightweight database for offline-first applications
- Sankore Compute: Distributed computing framework for low-bandwidth environments

Algorithm Layer

- UbuntuML: Machine learning library with communal loss functions
- AncestralNLP: Natural language processing for African languages
- Quantum-Griot: Quantum-inspired algorithms for complex systems

Governance Layer

- CommunityDAO: Digital autonomous organization templates for data cooperatives
- SovereignAudit: Algorithmic bias detection for African contexts
- EthicsOracle: AI ethics compliance checker

2. Defense Through Design Principles:

- Default Sovereignty: Systems designed to keep data local unless explicitly shared
- Graceful Degradation: Functionality maintained during internet outages
- Cultural Encryption: Knowledge representation that requires cultural context to decode

F. THE DIPLOMATIC DEFENSE PLAYBOOK

Objective: Strategies for navigating international AI governance and standards bodies.

1. African Bloc Strategy:
- Coordinate positions in ISO, IEEE, ITU AI standards committees
- Create African AI Standards Organization (AASO)
- Develop "Ubuntu Seal" certification for ethically aligned AI

2. Strategic Alliances:
- South-South technology sharing agreements
- Diaspora expert networks for technical assistance
- Academic partnerships that respect sovereignty

3. Counter-Narrative Campaigns:
- Document and publicize cases of digital colonialism
- Amplify African AI success stories
- Create African futurism media to counter dystopian narratives

G. THE SOVEREIGNTY STRESS TEST

Objective: Regular assessment of sovereign AI resilience.
Annual Sovereignty Audit Questions:
Technical Sovereignty (0-100)
- Can we maintain our AI systems if foreign vendors withdraw?
- Do we have capacity to audit and understand all AI systems in use?
- Are our data backups and recovery systems sovereign?

Economic Sovereignty (0-100)
- What percentage of AI value chain is locally owned?
- Do we have domestic AI investment and venture capital?
- Are we net exporters or importers of AI technology?

Cultural Sovereignty (0-100)
- Do our AI systems reflect African values and knowledge?
- Are we protecting indigenous knowledge from extraction?
- Is AI development inclusive of all African voices?

Strategic Sovereignty (0-100)
- Do we have sovereign capabilities in critical AI applications?
- Are we reducing dependencies on single foreign providers?
- Do we have contingency plans for AI-related crises?

Scoring:
- 80-100: Sovereign
- 60-79: Vulnerable
- Below 60: Colonial Dependency

H. THE WHISTLEBLOWER PROTECTION FRAMEWORK

Objective: Protect those who expose digital colonialism.
Protocol Includes:
- Anonymous reporting channels
- Legal defense fund
- International sanctuary network
- Digital security training
- Psychological support services

CONCLUSION: THE DEFENDER'S CREED
We stand as guardians at the dawn of Africa's digital age.
We remember that our data is the soil from which our future will grow.
We recognize that every algorithm encodes a worldview.
We understand that technological sovereignty is the continuation of liberation struggles by digital means.
We defend not against progress, but against predation.
We build not walls, but foundations.
We fear not the future, but the loss of our soul in reaching it.
Our tools are ready. Our resolve is firm. Our cause is just.
The defense begins now. The future is worth protecting.

APPENDIX I: ARMORY OF ARGUMENTS

Countering the Critics and Skeptics

This appendix provides the intellectual artillery to defend the revolutionary concepts in this book. Every criticism is an opportunity for education. Every skeptic is a future ally waiting to be awakened.

CRITICISM 1: "THIS IS JUST ANTI-WESTERN RESENTMENT DRESSED UP AS TECH CRITIQUE"

The Counter-Argument: The Architecture of Extraction

"This isn't about resentment; it's about mathematics. The colonial AI isn't 'Western' it's architecturallyextractive. The proof is in the data flows:

- 98% of Africa's data is stored offshore (UNCTAD)
- African nations pay $2-3 billion annually in cloud service fees (World Bank)
- For every $1 of foreign AI investment, $8-12 in value leaves the continent (AU Digital Economy Report)

This isn't emotion; it's accounting. We're not criticizing Western people—we're critiquing an extractive architecture that would be equally problematic if it originated anywhere else. The solution isn't to make Africans better consumers of colonial AI, but to build better AI architectures period."

Supporting Evidence:

- Reference Chapter 1's "Three Pillars of Digital Colonialism"
- World Bank Data: "The Digital Economy for Africa Initiative"

- UNCTAD's "Digital Economy Report 2019: Value Creation and Capture"

CRITICISM 2: "AFRICA SHOULD FOCUS ON BASIC NEEDS, NOT HIGH-TECH FANTASIES"

The Counter-Argument: The Leapfrog Imperative

"This criticism assumes technology is a luxury rather than the most powerful tool ever invented for solving basic needs. Consider:

- AI-powered diagnostics can reach 100x more patients than building physical hospitals
- Precision agriculture can triple yields without more land or water
- Predictive infrastructure maintenance saves billions lost to inefficiency

The choice isn't 'hospitals OR AI' it's 'hospitals AND AI that makes healthcare delivery 10x more efficient.' Africa cannot afford to solve 21st-century problems with 20th-century tools while the rest of the world advances. The 'basics' have changed digital infrastructure is now as fundamental as roads and electricity."

Supporting Evidence:

- WHO study on AI diagnostics in rural clinics
- FAO reports on AI and agricultural productivity
- Chapter 9's Prototype Nation cost-benefit analysis

CRITICISM 3: "THESE IDEAS ARE TOO PHILOSOPHICAL WHERE'S THE PRACTICAL IMPLEMENTATION?"

The Counter-Argument: Philosophy as the New Engineering

"Every technology is frozen philosophy. Silicon Valley's AI is frozen Cartesian dualism the belief in disembodied intelligence. Our architecture is frozen Ubuntu philosophy the understanding of relational intelligence.

But this isn't just theory:

- Chapter 8 provides complete mathematical formulations for communal loss functions

- Chapter 9 offers a 7-year implementation timeline with measurable milestones
- The Defenders Appendix provides policy templates and technical specifications

The most 'practical' thing we can do is fix the broken philosophical foundations before building more systems on them. Would you rather patch a collapsing building or fix the foundation?"

Supporting Evidence:

- Reference the complete technical architecture in Chapters 5-8
- Point to existing African AI successes: Ushahidi, M-Pesa, Zindi.ai
- Highlight the 34 specific "Sovereignty Protocols" throughout the book

CRITICISM 4: "THE QUANTUM-ANCESTRAL BRIDGE IS PSEUDOSCIENCE"

The Counter-Argument: The Coming Paradigm Shift

"This criticism assumes current Western scientific paradigms are complete. Yet leading physicists are increasingly acknowledging the limitations of materialist science:

- Nobel laureate Roger Penrose argues consciousness cannot be computed
- Physicist David Bohm's implicate order mirrors African concepts of interconnected reality
- The observer effect in quantum mechanics challenges Cartesian objectivity

We're not replacing science with spirituality we're expanding science to include phenomena that African traditions have understood for millennia. The 'pseudoscience' charge often masks a cultural bias against non-Western ways of knowing."

Supporting Evidence:

- Penrose, "The Emperor's New Mind"
- Bohm, "Wholeness and the Implicate Order"

- African philosophers: Mogobe Ramose on Ubuntu, Cheikh Anta Diop on African cosmology

CRITICISM 5: "THIS IS ISOLATIONIST AND ANTI-GLOBALIZATION"

The Counter-Argument: Sovereignty Enables Better Partnership

"Sovereignty isn't isolation it's the capacity for self-determination that makes genuine partnership possible. You can only have equal partnership between sovereigns.

Current 'globalization' in AI is like a partnership where one side brings all the ingredients, does all the cooking, sets the menu, and keeps 90% of the meal. We're proposing: Africa brings its unique ingredients (data, wisdom, context) to the kitchen and participates fully in the cooking and the feast.

This isn't anti-globalization it's pro-fairness. The current model is extractive globalization. We're proposing generative globalization."

Supporting Evidence:

- Reference successful sovereign partnerships: Rwanda's partnership with Zipline
- EU's GDPR as example of digital sovereignty enabling better global engagement
- Chapter 7's "Reciprocity Principle" in data sharing

CRITICISM 6: "AFRICA LACKS THE TECHNICAL CAPACITY FOR THIS"

The Counter Argument: The Myth of Technical Deficiency

"This argument confuses current resource distribution with innate capacity. Consider:

- Africa has the world's youngest population digital natives
- African engineers built M-Pesa, which revolutionized mobile banking
- African AI competitions like Zindi.ai attract thousands of brilliant data scientists

The 'capacity gap' is an investment gap, not a talent gap. When you've been told for centuries you can't build cathedrals, you don't suddenly realize you can't—you just stop trying. This book is the architectural blueprint that says: 'We can build cathedrals.'"

Supporting Evidence:

- GSMA report on African tech innovation
- Success stories: Andela, Flutterwave, Paystack
- Chapter 9's Ubuntu AI Academy curriculum

CRITICISM 7: "THIS SOUNDS LIKE ANOTHER FAILED AFRICAN RENAISSANCE PROJECT"

The Counter-Argument: The Tipping Point of Critical Mass

"Previous renaissance projects failed because they lacked either the technological means or the critical mass of awakened consciousness. We now have both:

- Digital connectivity has created pan-African consciousness
- The failure of neoliberal development models is obvious to all
- AI represents the greatest economic reorganization since industrialization

This isn't 1960s post-independence optimism it's 2020s technological inevitability. The question isn't whether Africa will shape AI, but whether it will do so consciously or reactively. This book is that conscious choice."

Supporting Evidence:

- Afrobarometer data on changing African consciousness
- The rise of pan-African tech ecosystems
- Successful precedents: African Union, AfCFTA

CRITICISM 8: "THE UBUNTU AI IS SOCIALLY CONSERVATIVE AND LIMITS INDIVIDUAL FREEDOM"

The Counter-Argument: Freedom Through Relationship

"Western individualism has created the most lonely, anxious, medicated population in history. The Ubuntu AI doesn't limit freedom it redefines it as 'freedom-in-relationship' rather than 'freedom-from-relationship.'

This isn't about social control it's about designing systems that don't optimize for individual addiction, polarization, and isolation. An AI that strengthens community bonds isn't conservative; it's literally conserving what makes us human.

The most advanced freedom is the freedom to participate in meaningful community, not the freedom to be a perfectly optimized consumer."

Supporting Evidence:

- Research on social connection and well-being
- Critique of attention economy models
- Chapter 5's mathematical formulations of communal flourishing

PREPARED RESPONSE TEMPLATES

For Academic Critics:

"Your critique assumes the framework of the very paradigm we're challenging. We're not playing the same game better we're playing a different game entirely. The question isn't whether our approach fits your existing metrics, but whether your metrics are adequate for measuring African realities."

For Policy Critics:

"The 'practical' approach you advocate has created the $2 billion annual data deficit we're now trying to fix. Sometimes the most practical solution requires philosophical depth. You can't solve a architectural problem with decorative solutions."

Forr Technical Critics:

"Your assertion that our approach isn't 'scalable' assumes scale means 'more of the same.' We're proposing scale means 'more diverse contexts working in harmony.' A forest scales differently than a monocrop plantation and is infinitely more resilient."

For Cultural Critics:

"Your concern about 'romanticizing the past' mistakes our project. We're not looking backward we're reaching back to fetch wisdom for a radically different future. The most advanced AI will look primitive next to the intelligence of a healthy ecosystem."

THE ULTIMATE RESPONSE

When all arguments fail, remember this foundational truth:

"They are critiquing from inside the cathedral. We are building from the forest. They cannot see what we see because their architecture limits their vision. Our work isn't to convince them it's to build so compelling an alternative that their criticisms become irrelevant."

This book isn't an argument to be won its a future to be built. The most powerful response to criticism is a working Prototype Nation that demonstrates these principles in practice.

DEFENSE AGAINST THE CRITICS: The Sankore Counter-Offensive

CRITIC 1: "This is just anti-Western sentiment dressed up as philosophy."

OUR RESPONSE:

"This isn't anti-Western it's pro-African. We're not rejecting technology; we're reclaiming its soul. When Europe had its Renaissance, it didn't apologize for drawing from Greek and Roman traditions. We're having our Digital Renaissance, drawing from Ubuntu, Ifá, and Kemetic wisdom. The question isn't why we're incorporating African philosophy, but why Western AI has so deliberately excluded it."

CRITIC 2: "These are just romanticized notions of African culture not practical engineering."

OUR RESPONSE:

"Tell that to the mycorrhizal networks that have managed forest ecosystems for 400 million years. Tell that to the Ubuntu principles that maintained social cohesion through centuries of adversity. We're not romanticizing we're learning from systems that have passed the ultimate stress test: survival. While Silicon Valley's 'move fast and break things' has broken democracies and mental health, African systems emphasize 'move wisely and build things that last.' Which approach seems more romantic now?"

CRITIC 3: "Africa should focus on catching up, not trying to leapfrog."

OUR RESPONSE:

"Catching up to what? A system that's hitting environmental limits, creating psychological distress, and concentrating wealth in fewer hands? We're not late to the party we're arriving just in time with the solutions to problems the first wave of AI created. While the West is trying to fix biased algorithms, we're building systems with justice baked in from the start. That's not leapfrogging that's evolving."

THE INTELLECTUAL SELF-DEFENSE MANUAL

When They Say: "This isn't rigorous computer science."
You Say: "The most rigorous computer science would acknowledge that current AI is built on incomplete foundations Cartesian dualism has been philosophically bankrupt for a century. We're doing the actual hard work of building AI on foundations that match what we know about embodied cognition, quantum physics, and complex systems. That's not less rigorous it's more."
When They Say: "This is just creating a different form of technological tribalism."
You Say: "Universal doesn't mean uniform. The current AI imposes one cultural framework globally and calls it 'universal.' True universality would be a system that can understand and respect multiple cultural contexts. We're building the first AI capable of genuine cultural intelligence that's the opposite of tribalism."
When They Say: "These ideas are too abstract to implement."
You Say: "The Prototype Nations chapter provides a seven-year implementation roadmap with specific technical architectures. We've outlined everything from the data cooperatives to the quantum-ancestral computing interfaces. The abstraction is in Western AI's refusal to acknowledge that intelligence can't be disembodied from culture and context."

THE CRITIC'S PLAYBOOK & OUR COUNTER-STRATEGY

Their Move #1: Appeal to Authority
"They'll cite Stanford, MIT, DeepMind as the 'real' experts."
Our Counter:
"The same institutions that gave us social media addiction, algorithmic bias, and surveillance capitalism? We'll take the authority of elders who maintained communities for millennia over engineers who can't predict the societal impact of their own code."
Their Move #2: The "Practicality" Trap
"This might work in theory, but the real world needs practical solutions."
Our Counter:
"What's more practical than systems that actually understand local context? A Western medical AI that misdiagnoses African patients because it was trained on European data? Or our context-aware systems built on African data for African bodies? Their 'practical' has been practically failing us for decades."
Their Move #3: The "Scale" Objection
"These small prototypes can't scale to compete with Google and OpenAI."
Our Counter:
"The mycelial network doesn't compete with the giant redwood—it enables entire forests to thrive. We're not building another corporate giant; we're growing an ecosystem. And ecosystems consistently outcompete and outlast monopolies in the long run."

EVIDENCE DOSSIER: PROVING THE POSSIBLE

Case Study 1: The M-Pesa Precedent
"They said African farmers wouldn't use mobile money. Now Kenya's M-Pesa handles 50% of GDP. Leapfrogging isn't theoretical we've done it before."
Case Study 2: Indigenous Knowledge Validation
"Western science is just catching up to what African traditional medicine knew about many plants. The science of ethnobotany now validates what elders have known for centuries."
Case Study 3: Ubuntu in Modern Governance
"South Africa's Truth and Reconciliation Commission applied Ubuntu principles to heal a nation—a more sophisticated approach to justice than purely punitive systems."

THE SANKORE DEBATE PLAYBOOK

Opening Gambit: Reframe the Conversation
Don't defend reframe. When they say "This isn't how AI is done," respond with: "That's exactly the point. We're showing how AI should be done."

Middle Game: The Evidence Hammer
Hit them with specific, undeniable examples of Western AI failure in African contexts:

- Medical AI that fails on darker skin
- Agricultural AI that recommends impossible practices
- Financial AI that excludes informal economies

End Game: The Visionary Close
"Your AI is built on 17th-century philosophy. Ours is built on wisdom that has sustained civilizations for millennia. The question isn't whether our approach is valid, but how long yours can remain relevant."

THE CRITIC'S WEAKNESSES & HOW TO EXPLOIT THEM

Weakness 1: They Can't Define Intelligence

They'll talk about benchmarks and metrics, but can't define what intelligence actually is.

Our Attack:

"Your AI can play chess but can't tell you why a community is suffering. Ours prioritizes understanding community flourishing. Which intelligence would you want making decisions about your family's future?"

Weakness 2: They're Culturally Illiterate

Most AI researchers can't name three African philosophers or understand non-Western epistemological traditions.

Our Attack:

"You're trying to build general intelligence while understanding only one cultural tradition. That's like trying to map the ocean while only knowing one cove."

Weakness 3: They're Defensive About Ethics

Every AI ethics conference is basically an admission that their current approach is ethically bankrupt.

Our Attack:

"You need entire conferences to discuss how to add ethics to your AI. We build it in from the foundation. Your approach is like trying to add structural integrity to a building after it's already built."

THE UNANSWERABLE QUESTIONS FOR OUR CRITICS

Ask them:
1. "How does your AI account for intergenerational responsibility?"
2. "What's the mathematical representation of community flourishing in your loss function?"
3. "How does your system preserve cultural context in its data processing?"
4. "What mechanisms ensure your AI doesn't optimize for individual benefit at community expense?"

THE SANKORE MANIFESTO BATTLE CRY

To Our Team:

They will come for us. The gatekeepers, the skeptics, the beneficiaries of the status quo. They will call us dreamers, radicals, unrealistic.

Good.

Every revolutionary idea was once called unrealistic. Every paradigm shift was resisted by those invested in the old paradigm.

They have the institutions. We have the truth.

They have the funding. We have the future.

They have the algorithms. We have the wisdom.

Let them criticize. Our Prototype Nations will be our proof. Our working systems will be our argument. Our communities flourishing will be our victory.

We're not just building AI. We're building a future where technology serves humanity instead of exploiting it. Where intelligence includes wisdom instead of just calculation. Where progress means everyone moves forward together.

The critics are welcome to their opinions. We're busy building the future they said was impossible.

THEY TALK. WE BUILD.

THEY CRITICIZE. WE CREATE.

THEY DEFEND THE PAST. WE'RE BUILDING THE FUTURE.

LET THEM COME.

www.ingramcontent.com/pod-product-compliance
Lightning Source LLC
LaVergne TN
LVHW090425210926
848480LV00002B/686
* 9 7 9 8 2 3 1 0 5 3 5 5 1 *